Cancer, What Now?

*Things To Know From The Start From Someone
Who Has Been There*

Morgan Maida

Prologue:

This book was written to help those newly affected by cancer. When I was diagnosed, I searched the internet and the library for a book to help me through this difficult time. I could not find one, so I wrote one in hopes of helping others. It is not designed to be a roadmap to cancer, but a helping hand. I hope to at least provide some comfort or insight to cancer patients, their families, and all affected by cancer.

Contents:

Section 1: The Diagnosis

The day you hear that you have cancer is one that you will probably never forget. It will also most likely be one of the hardest days you will ever have. There are many emotions when you hear you have cancer. I was mostly scared and I felt defeated. How could life have handed a 23-year-old Acute Myeloid Leukemia? I am sure you felt the same way. Maybe you were sad, mad, confused; all the emotions that you felt when you were told you have cancer are valid. You can't let someone tell you to stop crying. You will cry. You can't be scared to laugh- it is the best medicine. You have to still live your life. It is important to know that these emotions you felt then, and the emotions you feel now, are valid emotions. You are living with cancer, but cancer didn't come in and take over who you are. It is easy to let cancer become all-consuming. Don't let it. You are still you – you just now have cancer.

Cancer is a long journey. It is something that will take up a significant portion of your life and shape it in many ways. It is important that during this journey you understand that it is okay to cry. It's also okay to laugh and be happy, forgetting for a few moments what life has handed you. It is not a monotonous journey where everyday is the same. There are highs and lows. It is important to remember that it is okay to experience all of this. Our life cannot stop because of cancer. We cannot change who we are because of cancer. Cherish and enjoy all the other parts of life that are still happening. Cancer is only part of your life, you still can live it.

Section 2: The Hill

Early on in my cancer journey I had a conversation with myself. I put emotions aside and thought logically about what I was facing. I decided that cancer was a big hill put in front of me. It was tall, steep in parts, and there were going to be unforeseen obstacles as I began to climb. But, one thing I know to be true about hills is that they can be conquered. I may have to go over it, through it, or around it. I may have to do a combination of these. I may have to enlist help to get over some obstacles, or I might just need someone to say you can do it. No matter what the hill has to throw at us, there is another side and we will get there.

The Rules:
1. I will beat this. There is no option. Losing is not an option. You have to truly believe that you will beat this. Your mental attitude plays a huge role in your

cancer journey and having a positive outlook will do wonders.

2. I will not compare myself to where I was physically. You cannot compare your precancer self to yourself with cancer. Cancer takes a large physical toll on the body.

3. There is a hill, and I will succeed in climbing it no matter what it takes. The hill has unforeseen obstacles. You may have to adapt your plan of action to conquer these obstacles, but you can do it. You can climb the hill.

4. Don't get stuck in the "why me" trap. It is easy to ask ourselves "why did I end up with cancer, why am I here, why me". This idea of "why me" has no real answer. Maybe scientifically it does, but the concept of "why me" is detrimental to our progress. We are self-sabotaging by asking a question we will most likely never get an answer to. Cancer sucks, but you have to decide that you will beat it. Really believe that and that will carry you through cancer.

The Mindset

The first piece to success is our mindset. A positive mindset is our greatest ally and something we can control. There will be many things we cannot control during this journey, so having a piece that we are in total control over is huge. From day one, you have to truly believe that you can beat this. Taking it day by day is the first key. You can really look no further than today's challenges. These are in front of us, and we can complete them. Thinking about the journey as a whole can be overwhelming and make us feel like we aren't meeting these goals that were predetermined for us weeks ago. So, start with today. You can, and you will beat this.

Goal Setting

It is important to set attainable goals during this process. Some days getting up to shower is a hard to reach goal. Other days, you may be able to go on four walks and feel like a fifth. Each day is different. It is important to set goals daily. Every morning set at least one goal. It will push you to do at least one thing. One more step up that hill. Some days you may be able to set multiple goals and charge up that hill. Other days, one step forward will be all you can do. These goals must be short-term as the cancer journey changes daily. They must be set to challenge you, but also need to be set so they may be reached. Any step up, around, or through the hill is a step closer to the other side.

Taking The Win

I was a four-year college athlete who was on-the-go every weekend and generally an active person. Now, being able to put my heel on the ground is a greater success than hitting a walk-off home run. It was imperative for me to leave what I could do in the past alone. You cannot base physical successes during cancer on successes you had in life prior to cancer. Some days getting out of bed will be a success. Take that win. One day the doctors will walk in and say you get to go home and you are in remission. Take that win. You will need all the wins you can get. Celebrate the wins, and yes, I said celebrate, because even though you have cancer it is okay to be happy.

Section 3: Your Role

Note-taking

During this journey you will have many meetings and a whole lot going on. Have a notebook handy for everything. Write down questions that come to you or take notes as the doctors are talking so you can digest what he or she actually said. It is also extremely important to have someone with you during these meetings. There are times where you may go numb and not be able to listen after a certain word or phrase is said. It is important to have someone else there to continue listening for you. Afterwards, you and the other person or people can digest and talk to each other about the information.

You Are Your Best Advocate

During your time in the hospital and throughout the whole process you will constantly meet nurses, IV technicians, phlebotomists, doctors, therapists, nutritionists and so on. It is important that you ask questions and that you pay attention. If you don't feel comfortable with a certain nurse, ask for a new one. If you don't feel confident in the person trying to draw your blood, ask for someone else. You are a consumer in this process and you have a right to have the care that you see fit. If something seems off, ask. If you don't feel comfortable with something, say no. You have all these rights and you need to advocate for yourself in this process.

Feeling Independent

Just before I was diagnosed I was a fully independent, newly-retired college athlete. When I went into the hospital I needed help to even stand on my own two legs. It is hard to go from independent to dependent, but there are still ways to feel independent. Every person is going to gain their feeling of independence back a different way. It may be showering instead of a wipe-down bath. It may be taking a walk. It may be hooking up your own heart monitor (nurse supervised of course). Everyone will be different, but there are small ways you can gain your independence back, and if you revel in that feeling of being independent, find that task and repeat it each day. There is only so much we can control in the hospital, but what we can control is critical to our overall mental, emotional, and physical well-being.

How To Ask For Help

Everyone is different and how they want to be helped is different. You may want the nurses to help you with a difficult task or to take a shower, or you may want a loved one. Speak up and let people know what you prefer. They cannot read your mind and they cannot help you if they don't know what you want. Don't be afraid to ask a family member to help you shower instead of the CNA. If it makes you more comfortable, then it is what needs to occur. The best practice when asking for help is to know what you want and what you need. Then be direct. Don't beat around the bush and wait for someone to put words in your mouth. Voice what you need directly. Help others understand your needs so they may help you.

You Are Not Your Cancer

You are not your cancer. In no way, shape, or form are you now your cancer. There are times it will feel as if your identity has been stripped away and your identity is now your cancer, but it's not. You are still you. You are still the person you have always been, you just now have cancer to go along with everything you already are. Don't forget that you are you, and cancer is now something you have. Cancer does not define who you are. Keep being the person you are.

<u>Section 4: Your Well-Being</u>

The Mental, Emotional, Physical Aspect
Cancer will drain you in every way possible. The hospital will drain you. Talking to people will drain you. You will be mentally, emotionally, and physically drained during this process. That's okay, and it is okay to tell people to not visit, to tell the physical therapists "not today". Self-care is the most important part of this cancer journey. Your mind must be healthy and focused. If you rest your mind, you can use it for good and to have a positive mindset to climb up that hill.

It's Okay To Cry
You have to be positive and you have to be strong. However, you don't have to be positive and strong all the time. It is okay to just sit and cry and say "this sucks", because it does suck. You will have moments where you will have a full breakdown because cancer sucks. You have to let those emotions out. You have to acknowledge

that this sucks. People around you may think that this is a sign of defeat on your end, but it's not. It is an emotion and we will let it pass and continue onward. However, we can't allow these moments to take over our mindset. They need to be brief moments, and then we need to carry on. Keep charging up that hill, because someday soon we will be at the top.

Sleep All Day

Your cancer journey is a tiring one. Sleepless nights because of vital checks and chemo bag swaps. Sleepless days because of physical therapy, doctor visits and much more. There are days that you will be extremely tired. You will lay in bed and just sleep all day. That's okay. You will have those days and it is perfectly normal to have those days. Don't let the days become weeks. This is a marathon, not a sprint, and sometimes we just need to heal ourselves before we continue on up the hill. That's okay.

Laughter Is The Best Medicine

Sitting in a hospital room hooked up to IVs with nurses trouncing around you and the loudspeaker saying "Code Blue 10B3" does not lend itself to a happy environment. However, you have to make light of what is going on around you. Don't be afraid to laugh! It might be something terrible you're laughing at, but you're laughing. That is one of the best feelings. Don't let the hospital and the situation make you feel like you can't be you. It's okay to laugh, to make a joke, to have some joy in this terrible process. You have cancer, but it doesn't have to be all consuming all of the time, and it sure has no right to take away your laughter and joy.

Section 5: Family & Cancer

The Family

Your family will feel all types of emotions. They will be sad, angry, heartbroken, but it is important that during this time you understand it is not because of you. It is because of your cancer. But, yes, cancer is part of you now. It is really hard to watch your family cry because of you. To be hurt because of you. And to feel pain because of you. But it's not you. You will most likely rely on your family more during this time than ever before, but you need to be honest with them. You need to let them know what you need from them. They are your number one support system, but they can only support you so much, unless they have guidance from you on how you want to be supported. Talk to them, let them know what you need and above all love them. Love them so much for being there with you, for staying strong for you, and for supporting you.

Communicating Cancer

After being diagnosed you will need to communicate the diagnosis to friends, family, coworkers, *etc*. The phone calls are hard to make. The reactions, sometimes harder to take. Once the news about your cancer is out, you will most likely be overwhelmed with people wanting to help and wanting to support, and people wanting to visit. It will be overwhelming. I found a Facebook page to be a good communication tool to update everyone on your journey without being so overwhelmed with individual contacts. Trust me, a post is far easier than 60 texts. Every person will go through their own struggle while trying to communicate they have cancer. Be prepared to be overwhelmed, and create a plan to communicate updates that is easy for you.

The Dangers of The Internet

One of the first things you will probably do is turn to the internet for help to better understand what all is going on. Be careful. There is a lot of information on the internet, and it is not all pertinent to you and your cancer. The internet can be a great source of information, but you have to know how to read that information as it pertains to you. One of the biggest areas is survival rates. If you google a standard survival rate it is all encompassing of ages, ethnicities, genders, and probably not the most accurate for you. Cancer is also rapidly changing. A lot of the material about cancer that is available to the public through a google search is outdated. Ask your doctor any questions about your case because they can give you patient-specific responses.

Section 6: There Is No Roadmap

Cancer does not run on a schedule. Everyone's cancer is different. There is no roadmap in this situation and there is no timeline. Sometimes things will move quickly, other times you will be waiting around. It is all part of the journey. You can't look to other paths, yours will be different. Any timeline given will be for the best-case scenario. Prepare for bumps along the way. This is a marathon and not a sprint. The journey will take time, take the wins, believe in yourself, and kick cancer's butt.

A Few Extra Things To Know

- Smell tea bags while saline is being administered to prevent smelling the saline.
- Take your top five favorite foods and don't eat them while on chemo.
- Eat foods that you generally don't care for because they won't let you down with your changing taste buds.
- Keeping a daily journal helps to release thoughts and feelings.
- Take someone with you to every appointment.
- Be involved in your care.
- A pillow from home can be the difference for a good night's sleep.
- Always remember, you can do this!

About The Author

Morgan Maida was diagnosed with Acute Myeloid Leukemia at the age of 23. She wrote this book during her first two months of treatment. She hopes to provide a helping hand to those going through cancer. When she is not undergoing treatment or writing she loves to spend time with her family, friends, and dogs. Morgan hopes this book helps at least one person during their cancer journey.

Made in the USA
Middletown, DE
18 October 2022

12891702R00017